FOUNDERS

CROSS AND RESURRECTION
IN THE LIFE OF SOME FOUNDERS

FRANCIS OF ASSISI

TERESA OF AVILA

IGNATIUS OF LOYOLA

JOHN BAPTIST DE LA SALLE

ALPHONSUS LIGUORI

EDMUND RICE

THERESE COUDERC

ANTHONY MARY CLARET

JEANNE JUGAN

DON BOSCO

EDITED BY PATRICK LANGAN LC

Circle Press

Hamden CT

Scripture quotations are from the Jerusalem Bible,

copyright © 1966, 1967 and 1968

by Darton, Longman & Todd Ltd. and Doubleday & Company, Inc.

Used with permission.

Library of Congress Catalog card number: 97-67254

ISBN 0-9651601-1-4

Copyright © 1997 Patrick Langan LC

Printed in the United States of America

First Printing, May 1997

Circle Press

Hamden CT

"Let us lie in wait for the virtuous man,
since he annoys us and opposes our way of life,
reproaches us for our breaches of the law,
and accuses us of playing false to our upbringing.

"Before us he stands, a reproof to our way of thinking,
the very sight of him weighs our spirits down.

"Let us test him with cruelty and with torture,
and thus explore this gentleness of his
and put his endurance to the proof."

Wisdom 2: 12, 14, 19

❦

CONTENTS

CONTENTS

FOUNDERS

CROSS AND RESURRECTION IN THE LIFE OF SOME FOUNDERS

Key Insights

Holy Week 1997 provided me the time to do something I had been wanting to do for some time – read the lives of founders of religious families and try to see some of the constants of God's purifying action in their lives.

It was soon obvious that what I had in mind could not be done in a short time, but there was one factor that was immediately clear and unmistakable: the presence of the Cross, and concretely, the Cross of misinterpretation and defamation, with certain recurring characteristics:

* ❋ The accusations are always those best calculated in the culture of the day to damage the reputation of the founder.

* ❋ To any fair-minded observer at the time, the founder would at least seem suspect.

* ❋ The greater the impact the institute has on society, the more severe the attacks.

* In stormy times, the founder is the beacon that leads the ship to safe harbor.

* "The blood of martyrs is the seed of Christians," and the pesecution of founders is the seed of their order.

This book, a simple collection of true stories from the lives of several founders which illustrates the above, is the result.

Francis of Assisi

Francis kept having trouble sleeping. He was constantly restless, fascinated with knighthood, chivalry, and riches. One night, as he was lying ill in bed, his mind buzzing with the affairs of his father's business, he heard a sweet, mysterious voice say, "Francis, who can do more for you, a lord or his servant?"

Bewildered, Francis responded hesitantly, "The lord."

The voice continued, "Why then are you seeking the servant in place of the Lord?"

Francis was deeply shaken. He began to withdraw from his friends and stopped going to their banquets and parties which he had so enjoyed. He frequently came home dressed in rags, and sat with the beggars in the back of the church. He even stole and sold some cloth from his father's warehouse to help repair the small broken-down church of San Damiano.

Francis's strange behavior continued. He moved two miles outside Assisi and began to live near a tiny chapel called Portiuncula.

On the feast of St Matthias in 1209, Francis was attending Mass when he was struck to the heart by the Gospel: "Proclaim that the kingdom of heaven is close at hand.... Provide yourselves with no gold or silver, not even with a few coppers for your purses, with no haversack for the journey or spare tunic or footwear or a staff" (Matthew 10:7-19). As Mass was finishing, even while the priest was still at the altar, Francis began to slowly cast aside the remainder of his belongings.

Francis was now determined to live the absolute simplicity of the Gospel, calling it Lady Poverty. He would renounce the goods of the world and seek only the treasures of heaven. His way of life began to attract certain prominent men of Assisi, who sold their possessions to be his companions in poverty.

Francis decided to go to Rome. He had written a rule of life centered on absolute poverty and gospel simplicity, but he wanted it confirmed by the highest authority of the Church.

Francis and his companions presented themselves first to Bishop Guido of Assisi. He in turn introduced the brothers to a friend of his, the highly influential Cardinal Ugolino, nephew of Innocent III and later himself Pope Gregory IX. Intrigued by Francis and his followers, Cardinal Ugolino began to investigate their intentions and prospects. No one had ever before seen a rule like the one Francis had devised. It lacked the normal prescriptions for community life.

In particular, the radical poverty that Francis and his followers lived seemed suspicious to Cardinal Ugolino. At the time there was a sect called the Albigensians teaching that the devil was a rival god to the Christian God and had imprisoned the good human soul in evil matter. For the Albigensians, salvation for the soul consisted in liberation from material things. Since Francis was from Assisi, a center of the Albigensians, his radical approach to evangelical poverty immediately brought him under suspicion of heresy.

Recent history also caused some concern. In 1179, Peter Valdes had obtained permission from Pope Alexander III to preach and live in apostolic poverty. In 1184, Valdes and his followers were placed under a ban as rebels against the Church. It was an experience no one in Rome wanted to repeat.

Despite his concerns, Cardinal Ugolino arranged for Francis to meet Pope Innocent III in the Lateran Palace. The Pope was not well disposed. Francis walked into the Lateran unceremoniously and went up to the Pope. Seeing the poor, ragged tunic, the tangled locks, and the great black eyebrows, Innocent pretended to take him for a swine herder.

"Leave me alone with your rule!" he exclaimed. "Go find your pigs, and preach to them all you want!"

Francis was not in the least put out. Instead, he went to the nearest pig sty, smeared mud all over himself, and then presented himself to the Pope once more.

Innocent was impressed, and after thinking it over he regretted having given him such a rough reception. Before sending him away to get washed, he promised him another audience. On the second occasion, the cardinals were also present as Francis presented his program.

Innocent listened intently, and when Francis had finished, he said, "My dear son, this life you and your brothers lead seems too severe. Seeing your enthusiasm, I certainly do not doubt that you are all willing to live it. But what of those who will come after you? They may not have the same zeal."

Francis had only this answer: "Holy Father, I trust in my Lord Jesus Christ. He has promised us eternal life and the bliss of heaven; he would not deny us the little we need to sustain our life on earth."

Francis and the brothers left the pope, who discussed the matter before the cardinals in the next consistory. Most of the cardinals opposed Francis' radical poverty .At this point, a cardinal who had been won over to Francis's way of thinking said, "These men only want to live the gospel. If we declare it impossible, then we declare that the gospel cannot be followed, and so insult Christ and the gospel." Hearing this, the cardinals decided to postpone judgment, and Francis was again invited to the Lateran.

The night before this next meeting, the pope had a curious dream. He stood looking out over the Lateran Church and watched with fear as the proud building shook, the tower swung, and the walls began to crack. Suddenly, a small common-looking man came towards the Lateran. He was dressed in peasant garb, was barefoot, and wore a rope around his waist for a belt. Rushing to the falling Church, he set his shoulder in under the wall and with a mighty push straightened the whole falling church, so that it again stood aright. The pope recognized the man as Francis of Assisi.

The next day, the pope gave Francis an oral approval of his rule, but the approval was never put into writing.

The Rule

Cardinal Ugolino continued to maintain contact with the group, often attending the twice-yearly gatherings of the Franciscans at Portiuncula. These were informal events involving thousands of the friars. Like everything else Francis did, these meetings had not the slightest shade of formal organization. No provisions were made for food, no formal agenda was arranged. The friars would have gone without food if not for the spontaneous generosity of the people of Assisi, who brought cartloads of fruit, wine, cheese, fish, and bread.

While at such meetings, Cardinal Ugolino saw that the friars had tremendous potential for building up the Church, but he was disheartened to see this potential go unchanneled. Ugolino knew that all of their work could be better organized and directed if their founder would only take up one of the more conventional rules. Many times he tried to convince Francis to adopt the Benedictine rule for his friars, but the cardinal always received the same response: "The rule came to me from Jesus himself."

Friars like Brother Elias of Cortona shared Cardinal Ugolino's vision for the brethren: they should be a regular order, with papal privileges like the ones the Dominicans enjoyed. That would bring an end to many of the difficulties that so often accompanied their journeys, they argued. To the practical-minded churchmen of the day, Francis's ideas of absolute poverty seemed like mere dreams. Consequently, dissension began to spread through the ranks.

Francis left in June 1219 for Egypt and Syria, leaving two vicars in charge at Assisi. While convincing rumors circulated that Francis was dead, a victim of disease somewhere in the Orient, the vicars introduced innovations which would bring stability and order to the Franciscan lifestyle. The practice of poverty was relaxed, and the friars began to live along the lines of conventional religious orders.

Francis returned from his journey to find his friars dwelling in comfortable homes and calling objects "mine." Passing through Bologna, he lodged with Dominican friars rather than with his own, and upon reaching Assisi he resigned active control of his order. Six months after his abdication, Brother Elias became minister general and continued to actively promote the changes so alien to the spirit of Francis.

Francis Prevails

In 1221, Francis set about to revise the rule, hoping that a revised rule approved by the pope would maintain his own vision for the community's spirit. The revision compromised none of the original inspiration he had received from God, but he knew that it would not be well received.

After spending the winter working, he handed the sole manuscript to Brother Elias for distribution. Elias took the rule, promising to examine it with the brethren. Days passed without a response, and Francis finally visited Elias to obtain an answer. Inexplicably, the rule had been lost. They had looked for it everywhere, but to no avail. "Lord," Francis cried, "didn't I tell you that they wouldn't trust you?"

Francis was resolute and rewrote the rule. Bypassing Elias, he presented it to a gathering of the brothers at Pentecost. The friars supported the rule, and Francis submitted it to Rome. The pope formally approved the rule on November 29, 1223.

Francis of Assisi

Lifetime: *Born in 1181, died in 1226 at the age of 45*

Order: *Franciscans(Friars Minor)*

Founded: *Assisi,1209, at the age of 28*

Mission: *The itinerant preaching of the gospel and the living of absolute poverty in charitable brotherhood*

Impact: *Francis's spirit of detachment and poverty has influenced more than 30 male orders and 300 provinces of female religious who today claim him as their spiritual father. In addition to the Friars Minor, Francis also founded the Third Order for laity who wished to lead a contemplative life in the world. Francis has been hailed as the most influential saint in post-apostolic times.*

Quote: *"I will go and entrust the Order of Friars Minor to the holy Roman Church. Under her protection no harm will come upon the Order, and the sons of Satan will not trample over the vineyard of the Lord with impunity. Our holy Mother will herself imitate the glory of our poverty.... The sacred observance of evangelical poverty will ever flourish before her, and she will never allow the fragrance of our good name and holy life to be destroyed."*

Teresa of Avila

As the fresh dawn rose over the Spanish hills, all the bells of the many churches and convents of the city began to announce the beginning of the new day. Early risers in the suburb of Saint Roch at the northern fringe of Avila must have heard a startling sound. An unaccustomed tinkling was coming from the doorway of the small house where mysterious activity had lately been reported.

None of the great bells of Avila, not even the grandiose chimes of San Gil, Santa Ana, and Las Gordillas, evoked as much emotion as did the humble bells of San Jose for those who rang them for the first time.

The ceremony followed immediately lest someone interrupt at the last moment. Teresa presented her four candidates to Fr Daza, who gave them their habits in the name of the bishop. Fr Daza then put on his vestments and began saying Mass. At last the Blessed Sacrament was present in the humble abode. As the four novices in their new robes were formally encloistered and given their names in religion, the Discalced Carmelites came into being.

Teresa and her four daughters were alone at last in the blessed solitude they had desired. The prayers of so many days and nights were answered and fulfilled. "In the world you shall have distress, but have confidence: I have overcome the world."

Unwelcome Intrusion

The next day the mayor of Avila, Señor Suarez, summoned the city council to discuss the disturbance which had the whole town talking. It had become known that certain women claiming to be Carmelite nuns had occupied the house of San Jose. As if Avila needed another convent! Were there not enough monasteries and convents to begin with?

Let no one misunderstand. The people of Avila loved religion. Nearly every important family had one or more members in one of the many religious communities. The people generously supported the religious communities and would never turn their back on a servant of God in need. But Avila was not a wealthy town, and the people could give no more; this new convent was a burden that simply could not be shouldered. The council decided that all the learned men of Avila must be summoned.

In the meantime, the mayor went to the new convent and

knocked on the door, demanding to be admitted. A terrified novice spoke through the door, asking what he wanted, while a crowd of officials and townspeople looked on to see what would happen. The mayor replied that the people did not desire another convent in the city; they must leave at once and return to their homes.

"We will leave only by command of our superior, Teresa," said the nun.

"Open the doors or I will break them down!"

In response, the women barricaded themselves in as best they could, using pieces of boards left over from recent repairs. They were determined to resist. The mayor was furious, and would undoubtedly have forced his way in had he not seen the Blessed Sacrament on the altar near the front entrance. Being a good Catholic, he desisted and went away, but not without leaving some parting warnings.

The city council met on Wednesday morning and appointed a delegate to give the bishop an account of the city's reaction against the new convent. They wanted the bishop to know that they were resolved to appeal to King Philip II and the Royal Council if necessary. On Saturday plans were made to rally the city's public opinion leaders to come to an assembly at the Council Hall the following day. The bishop was invited to attend, and all the learned men of Avila were summoned.

Avila Outraged

It was a solemn and imposing assembly that came together after Mass that Sunday. All the nobility and learned men of Avila were represented in the colorful throng, and at the heart of it all were the city officials in brilliant costumes braided with gold. Indeed, the city could have produced no greater demonstration if menaced by flood, pestilence, or invasion, rather than by five poor women who wanted only to pray and to eat as little as possible.

The mayor was eager to begin; he had an arsenal of arguments prepared. "We are gathered here, illustrious gentlemen, for something which could easily be decided without the opinion of so many eminent people. But I wanted to make use of your presence so that my actions, having the approval of people held in highest esteem, may have greater weight.

"We are all acutely aware of the new convent of Discalced Carmelites. But this is not an ordinary convent: it is an innovation and should make us wary. Such things cause confusion; they disturb the minds of the people; they set tongues in motion, foment murmuring, and engender disorder. This is true of innovations in general; the present one, however, is all the more dangerous since it wears the outward appearance of great piety.

"I submit that in this city it is not only expedient but rather a matter of urgent necessity to prevent new religious foundations. Although Avila is among the noblest cities of Spain, it is by no means among the richest, and it already has as many monasteries and convents as it can prudently support. In the end, what is given to a convent is taken away from the rest of the city. This convent is founded without income, without dowry, and with the presumption that it will never have any.

"Gentlemen, this is nothing other than a compulsory tax. It is certain to take money out of our purses and food from our mouths. What heart could endure to see some poor servants of God perishing of hunger? Would we not be compelled to take bread from our children in order to share it with them?

"Furthermore, if the city is responsible for all its citizens and convents, how is it possible that a foundation is made without approval? What government would endure such contempt for authority?

"Moreover, how do we know that this foundation is not some fraud, or a deceit of the devil? They say that their founder has revelations and a very peculiar spirit. That very fact frightens me, and it ought to make us reflect deeply, since in these times we have seen deceits and illusions among women.

"It is not my object to accuse these religious of fraud. Nevertheless, I would advise against admitting innovations, letting convents multiply, and allowing them to be established without the permission and knowledge of the city. We have a right to inquire from experts whether it is a question of the Lord's service. This is my opinion; I hope that it will be approved by all the learned and experienced men that are here assembled."

When the mayor finished, the bishop's representative rose to address the assembly. He informed them that the foundation had been made with the consent of His Excellency and then read the document of Pope Pius IV under which the consent had been given.

It was certainly a blow to the mayor's case, but he stood his ground and asked for other opinions. The people remained in agreement with him, and one speech followed another. The Inspector of Wells testified that material damage would be done to the whole community, for the convent shut off the sunlight from a small arched structure which sheltered several springs for public use. With the sunlight blocked, the water would freeze in winter and be of no use.

As the proceedings continued, the general indignation against the five Carmelites mounted in a violent crescendo. When Teresa heard about it later, she was surprised that the angry mob had not gone then and there to demolish her house.

A Single Supporter

There was only one man who dared to speak out against the hysteria of the community: thirty-four year old Fr Bañez.

"It may seem rash to oppose so many illustrious personages whose arguments and reasonings are so well thought out, but my own conscience urges me to support the new convent of Discalced Carmelites. My words are free from passion and are unbiased, for I have never spoken with nor met the founder, nor discussed her foundation in any way.

"I admit that a convent such as this is a novelty, and as such it has produced the effects that innovations usually do among the multitude. But this is no reason why it should produce these same effects in grave and prudent councils, for not every new thing deserves our censure.

"Consider the immense good done for society by the great religious orders; were they founded any other way? Did not every reform have a similar beginning? Surely nothing could be improved if we all surrendered to a cowardly fear of everything new. What is introduced for the greater glory of God and the reform of morals should not be labeled innovation or invention, but rather the renewal of virtue, which never changes.

"If the trees are new when they are seen in spring, and the sun is new when it rises each morning, is it such a great problem that religious orders also renew themselves from time to time? Which is worse: that they lose their ancient splendor or that they rejuvenate it?

"I do not approve of the rash multiplication of religious orders, but let us not make this our sole criterion for judgment. The cities are full of lost people; the streets swarm with insolent and lazy men, and with boys and girls given over to vice. Is our nation so greatly injured and burdened by a few nuns tucked away in a hole-in-a-corner commending themselves to God? Allow me to say that the prestige of such an important city as this one seems lessened when it holds so solemn a meeting for so light a reason."

But the council was already resolved, and voted to send a proposal to the bishop asking that the Blessed Sacrament at the convent be consumed and the place closed.

The bishop stood by Teresa. He sent Fr Daza to represent him at yet another meeting to remind the city that the convent had been established with papal and episcopal permission. Fr Daza added that he himself had presided at the opening ceremonies and had said the first Mass.

The leaders of the opposition were still dissatisfied, and the city council sent a delegate to Madrid to complain to the Royal Council.

A Tempting Compromise

Summer was turning to autumn, and still the conflict raged. At last, the city council agreed to allow the convent to remain on the condition that Teresa have it endowed. It was an excruciating temptation. She had not wanted any monetary endowments so as to live the vow of poverty more perfectly.

On the other hand, she was weary from months of anxiety and trouble, sorry for her friends who had endured so much, and concerned that perhaps she was being misled by pride. Her friends argued that if she accepted an endowment, she could easily give it up later and return to the original plan. Teresa was prepared to accept the city's reasonable compromise and sign a contract the next day.

Teresa awoke the next morning and changed her mind. She immediately told her lawyer to continue with the lawsuit. Her perplexed friends kept trying to work out a solution, but Teresa stubbornly refused every offer of compromise.

Her friends were bewildered. "What has gotten into her head all of a sudden?"

"What do you mean—she's just being her old capricious self. She's far too proud to change her mind now."

"It's enough to try the patience of a saint! I went to so much trouble to arrange that compromise. The sheer ingratitude is what bothers me most."

The lawsuit dragged on through the long winter. But at last, a turning point was reached when Fr Pedro Ibañez arrived in town. It was he who had first written to Rome for the bull of authorization.

Fr Ibañez was universally loved and respected in Avila. When it became known that he was on the side of the new convent, the opposition began to melt away. By spring it had dwindled to nothing.

Teresa was not being as unreasonable as it seemed. The night before she was going to sign the contract, Our Lord appeared to her in a dream, telling her not to do it; if she began with an endowment, she would be unable to renounce it later. It turned out that the convent of San Jose did not take anything away from Avila either spiritually or financially, as the flocks of pilgrims that visit each year still testify. And from that time on, the name of Avila has been inseparably linked to a woman called Teresa.

Teresa of Avila

Lifetime: Born in 1515, died in 1582 at the age of 67

Order: Discalced Carmelites

Founded: Avila, Spain, 1562, at the age of 47

Mission: Prayer and contemplation

Impact: Teresa originally intended to found only one convent, but requests from bishops encouraged her to establish additional convents of cloistered Carmelite nuns. She spent the remainder of her life traveling throughout Spain founding convents. By the time of her death, fifteen had been founded.

Quote: "I went to trial pleased enough that I had suffered something for the Lord, for I did not find that I had done anything wrong against His Majesty or the Order. Rather I had tried to strengthen it with all my powers, and I would gladly die for it, since my whole desire was that it carry on with all perfection. I called to mind the judgment passed on Christ, and saw what a trifle this one was. I told my faults as one who was guilty, and so it seemed to everyone who did not know all the causes. The provincial reprimanded me, though not with as much rigor as some had told him I deserved. I did not try to excuse myself, for I was resigned to it; rather, I asked him to forgive me and punish me, and not to be displeased with me."

Ignatius of Loyola

Quirino Garzonio was apprehensive. The situation in Rome had changed drastically for his long-time friend Ignatius of Loyola. When Ignatius and his companions had first come to Rome, their influence upon the people had been immediate and widespread. Jesuits were teaching at the Sapienza, preaching in the churches, and revitalizing clergy and laity alike.

But all this began to change with the arrival of Fra Agostino Mainardi. This Augustinian friar had arrived in Rome while the pope was away, and had obtained permission to preach. His eloquence immediately gained him a popular following. He began to warn the people about Ignatius Loyola and his companions. He informed them that the Jesuits had been driven out of Paris on a charge of heresy and were fleeing everywhere from the Inquisition. He was aided in his plan by Michael Navarro, a passionate young man who had actually spent some time with Ignatius and his group, so he had the convincing air of one who knew the group from the inside.

Three of Agostino's companions joined Navarro in warning important political and ecclesiastical leaders about Ignatius and his companions. The reports spread like wildfire, and the faithful began to shun the accused men. Even the authorities were preparing to condemn the Jesuits.

A Favorable Meeting

Now Quirino's relative Cardinal John de Cupis, the head of the Sacred College, was trying to convince him to break off all relations with Ignatius. "They say he is fleeing from the Inquisition," the cardinal insisted.

"He would not be the first holy man wrongly accused," retorted Quirino.

The cardinal looked at Quirino pityingly and said, "You have been enchanted by this man. You do not know what I have heard about him; there are convincing accusations against him. Be assured, this man is very different from what you suppose."

The cardinal continued matter-of-factly, "At the very least, he is under a cloud and it is no longer prudent to continue dealing with him. You have to understand, my name is being associated with you."

Quirino insisted that it was unjust to denounce a person without a hearing. He begged the cardinal to speak with Ignatius himself and learn the real situation. Cardinal de Cupis agreed to send for Ignatius, declaring pointedly, "I shall treat him as he deserves."

The meeting happened as the cardinal had promised, both men met for over two hours while Quirino waited anxiously outside the room. In the course of their meeting, Cardinal de Cupis was completely won over to Ignatius's cause.

An Initial Victory

Ignatius then went straight to the Governor of Rome and expressly demanded a formal hearing. The Governor consented and fixed a time for them to appear.

While awaiting the hearing, Ignatius obtained a letter Michael Navarro had written one of his friends while still on good terms with the Jesuits. This letter praised Ignatius and the Jesuits, utterly contradicting all that Navarro had sworn under oath.

When the hearing began, Ignatius confronted Navarro with the letter, asking if he acknowledged writing it. When he replied that he did, Ignatius read it publicly; the accuser, confounded by his own words, had nothing more to say. Navarro had proved himself to be a false accuser, and he was given the customary punishment of exile.

Trying to win a definitive victory, Ignatius insisted that the other three accusers bring their cases before the Governor. They immediately changed their stories, and said they only had the highest praise for Ignatius. At this, the governor was satisfied, and the case was closed.

Ignatius, however, was still far from pleased with the outcome. He knew that without a definitive verdict of his innocence, the apostolic activities of his group would remain open to suspicion. He still had to find a way to clear his name.

A Step Further

Many of his companions advised Ignatius to let the matter rest, but he stubbornly refused. "We know," he wrote, "that this will not prevent us being blamed in the future, and besides, it is not what we want. We have only wished to save and protect our honor, and, at the same time, the sound doctrine and way of life we have embraced. If we are represented as ignorant, stupid people, without eloquence, or even vile, unsettled, or deceivers, we will never complain. But what afflicts us is that they represent the doctrine we preach as erroneous, and the life which we lead as bad: now these two things affect Jesus Christ and his Church."

Ignatius and his companions set to work mustering support for their cause. Contacting authorities in the cities where they had been working, they requested testimonies about the young company's life and doctrine, and received favorable responses from Siena, Bologna, and Ferrara.

When Pope Paul III returned to Rome on July 24 from his trip to Nice, Ignatius did everything possible to secure an audience with him. In late August, the pope moved to Frascati and consented to see Ignatius there.

Ignatius stated his case before the pope. He told of his past troubles with people who resented his work and brought the Inquisition against him. He explained that he had been examined by the Inquisition in Spain, in France, and in Italy. On each occasion the verdict had been in his favor, but the magistrates kept leaving room for doubt.

"Holy Father, is this justice?" he cried. "In all three places I was told, 'What you have done is not wrong, but do not do it again.' They tell us we are innocent, but we should hold our tongues. We are not to be attacked, but neither can we speak out in our defense."

The pope listened and in the end gave orders for a fresh trial before the governor. When sentence on Ignatius was passed, it not only cleared him of all faults, but also went on to praise the company for the excellence of their lives and the doctrines they preached.

Ignatius would later say that this was the worst storm in the foundation of the Society of Jesus.

Ignatius of Loyola

Lifetime: Born in 1491, died in 1556 at the age of 65

Order: Society of Jesus (Jesuits)

Founded: Paris, France, 1541, at the age of 50

Mission: Preaching and evangelization according to the will of the pope

Impact: There were 938 members at the time of Ignatius's death. During the Counter-Reformation they played an extremely prominent role in revivifying Catholicism spiritually and intellectually, halting the advances of Protestantism, and regaining lost ground in the Low Countries, France, and Central and Eastern Europe.

Quote: "Dear Lord, teach me to be generous.

Teach me to serve you as you deserve.

To give and not to count the cost.

To fight and not to heed the wounds.

To toil and not to seek for rest.

To labor and not to seek reward save that

of knowing that

I do your will,

O God."

John Baptist de la Salle

"If he is robbing us of our students," said the old supervisor, leaning forward in his chair, "then go to his school, take all his desks, and throw them out on the street. When you are finished, let me know so we can move on to the next step."

When everyone had left, Claude Joly sat back in his chair. At eighty-three, the superintendent of the Paris fee-paying schools was still full of vigor. His life had been a constant fight against despotism of every kind, and now it was his duty to safeguard the interests of the fee-paying schools.

The case of the Christian Brothers school on Du Bac Street was a perfect example of an intolerable abuse of authority by Father de la Salle. For some time, complaints about the Christian Brothers had been reaching the ears of the superintendent, and he watched with increasing alarm the growth of dc la Salle's work.

These schools were attracting all the children of the area. The teachers of the fee-paying schools were left without students and without the possibility of a livelihood. There would have been no problem if every boy in the Christian Brothers schools were poor and incapable of paying. However, it was said that some parents who could afford to pay were sending their children to these charity schools anyway. Fr de la Salle was making no effort to be selective, and for that reason these schools were a menace.

Moreover, the Christian Brothers were threatening time-honored, traditional methods of teaching. All the students were now being organized into one classroom, all with the same textbooks and studying the same lesson at once. Fr de la Salle even dared to undermine the very language of education itself. For centuries, teaching had always been in Latin. Yet Fr de la Salle was now introducing the modern language ahead of Latin, saying he wanted to make sure the students mastered their own language first.

Furthermore, some former Christian Brothers had complained that the work was too hard and that discipline was not the way it should be. Some even walked out and lodged official complaints.

Joly only saw trouble if the Christian Brothers were left unchecked. The worthy supervisor knew that he alone could stop Fr de la Salle before he went too far.

Claude Joly was in a strong position. In his twenty years as superintendent, he had won the confidence of the fee-paying schools' teachers; they looked upon him as their champion. He was a faithful guardian of the privileges of the guild, and he knew his teachers resented Fr de la Salle's success. He could count on their support in any action he might take to protect their rights. The time was ripe to intervene before these opportunists went any further.

After the raid was made on the school in Du Bac Street, a formal condemnation was launched against the founder ordering his schools to be closed. Claude Joly filed a lawsuit and awaited the decision of the law courts. He was confident of an easy victory, for he knew that Fr de la Salle detested lawsuits.

The Birth of the School

In fact, Fr de la Salle had never wanted to start a congregation. He had been minding his own business, working on his doctorate in theology at the University of Rheims. He was happy being a priest and loved his studies. Independently wealthy, he supported his family at his large house. His life seemed to be falling into place just as he wanted; that is, until he met Adrien Nyel.

Nyel was a man with a vision. He had spent his life in the midst of children and felt moved to establish a school for boys who could not afford an education. In his search for help, he had been referred to Fr de la Salle and went to him for advice.

Fr de la Salle received his visitor politely into his parlor and listened to his proposal with interest, but he immediately saw all the difficulties involved. He realized how a new foundation of this kind would not only interfere with the already established educational structure of the city but would also meet a wall of general indifference. He had seen the difficulties which had beset the foundation of a girls' school, and he foresaw that opposition to a boys' school would be far more formidable.

There were already official schoolmasters in the city; what would they say when they saw their position threatened? The Archbishop had been generous and considerate in the foundation of a school for girls, but would he extend his interest to a new school for boys?

Although Fr de la Salle did not want to get involved, he was deeply impressed with Nyel. He prayed over the matter and sought advice from the pastor of St Maurice, who was already considering opening a free school in his parish. Moreover, Providence had just sent money to support such a project.

Fr de la Salle was satisfied. He had found the contact Nyel needed to start his project. Nyel would work well at St Maurice, and Fr de la Salle could withdraw once more to pursue his studies. But Nyel wrote to him often and visited him frequently to discuss the problems and difficulties of the work.

Word of the new school began to circulate, and soon a wealthy woman from a neighboring parish wanted to found a school similar to the one at St Maurice. Nyel was an immediate enthusiast. He went to visit her, painting a glowing picture of what was being achieved and assuring her that Fr de la Salle would gladly support any such project.

But Fr de la Salle was not to be rushed. He saw Nyel's danger: increasing foundations without consolidating the ones that were already working. However, he did not want to get in the way of any good that might come of it. Fr de la Salle met with her and reluctantly agreed to get involved. When she died six weeks later, her heirs faithfully carried out her wishes to found the school. In September of 1679 the new school opened. Shortly afterwards, there was another foundation, and then another, and another, until soon Fr de la Salle was entangled in a work in which he had never intended to take part.

Teacher Trouble

He now found himself in charge of several schools as well as the formation of their hastily recruited teachers, qualified men, but rude and ill-mannered. Fr de la Salle was convinced that good manners were a necessary part of being a Christian role model, but how could he refine the teachers? He thought the whole matter over, and on the principle of Mohammed and the mountain, he decided to bring them to his table.

They should come twice a day and have their meals in silence while one of them read aloud. When the meal was over, Fr de la Salle would give them a short spiritual talk on the great work to which they had devoted themselves and the various means of preparing themselves for it.

His family members were not at all pleased with his guests, and his brothers complained. They pointed out that even though the house was his property, he might at least take into consideration his own brothers who also lived there.

To complicate matters further, the rent on the house leased for the schoolmasters was about to expire. Fr de la Salle could have its lease renewed, or he could follow Nyel's suggestions and take the teachers into his own home. It was a matter that Fr de la Salle did not feel competent to judge for himself, so he left for Paris to consult Fr Barre, a priest renowned for his holiness and learning who had himself founded several schools.

Fr de la Salle laid the whole problem before him. Fr Barre, in turn, told Fr de la Salle that God had chosen him to do this work, and that the obstacles were means God used to strengthen it.

"The greatest designs of God upon a soul," he exhorted Fr de la Salle, "are only achieved through opposition. Exterior and interior trials invigorate the soul. As you could get no wine without crushing it in the winepress, neither could a soul produce any good work unless it has been on the winepress of temptations, persecutions, trials, and afflictions. The perfect religious ought to be like the cock on the church steeple: it turns with every wind without ever coming from under the cross." Fr de la Salle resolved to follow his friend's advice and returned home to Rheims.

Making promises to God is not that difficult; keeping them is. The difficulties for Fr de la Salle were only beginning, for shortly afterwards, news arrived that Adrien Nyel had died suddenly in Rouen. But Fr de la Salle had already made his decision. In June, on the feast of his patron saint, he took the whole community into his house.

His relatives protested: "It was bad enough to have them at table! Does he now intend to bring them into our family home?" Some said he was mad, that he had lost all feelings of affection. Others told him he had lost his dignity as a priest. The whole idea was disgracefully wrong, and Fr de la Salle had no answer. He would listen to them courteously, kindly, and patiently, and when they had finished, he would return to his work of forming the teachers.

His family walked out.

His relatives had left him, his friends were skeptical, and now even the men for whom he had sacrificed so much began to grumble. His very regularity became their complaint.

The teachers had volunteered to teach, not to become religious. Yet, they found themselves living in a house where, without any doubt at all, they were subject to the discipline of a religious congregation.

Fr de la Salle did not despair. He knew that if the schools were not the work of God, then they deserved to perish. If, on the other hand, they were God's work, then the power of God would protect them: all would end well.

A Second Beginning

When one group of teachers departed, another group quickly took their place. These were men who had received a solid education, Christian teachers in the best sense of the word. He and some of his companions vowed never to abandon the work even if they were reduced to living on bread alone, but their resolve was soon put to the test.

It was at this point that Claude Joly filed his lawsuit to close the schools. Fr de la Salle had done everything possible to avoid an open conflict, but Joly would not be moved. Suppressing his deep longing to leave the congregation and go back to his books, Fr de la Salle went on a pilgrimage with all the brothers to the Shrine of Notre Dame des Vertus, where St Vincent de Paul had often gone to pray in times of need at the little church of Aubervilliers.

After praying for guidance and the wisdom to know what to do, he decided to fight for the rights of his congregation and his students.

Claude Joly soon discovered that he had underestimated Fr de la Salle. The priest showed he could present his arguments effectively once he set his mind to the task, since rhetoric had been part of his education. He stated his case so forcibly and with such precision that within a short space of time the lawsuit was decided in his favor.

Joly carried the appeal to Parliament. Fr de la Salle defended the case himself and won. The schools were reopened, discipline was tightened, and each morning the improvement in the student's behavior became more and more marked. People began to notice the change, and the general public became more sympathetic on account of the good being done in the schools.

John Baptist de la Salle continued to guide the Christian Brothers, establishing primary schools on an extensive scale in order to offer the people a Christian education. When it became obvious that the Christian Brothers alone could not supply the many demands, he began to train lay people for the work, founding the first training college for teachers in the history of education.

John Baptist de la Salle

Lifetime: Born in 1651, died in 1719 at the age of 67

Order: Christian Brothers

Founded: Rheims, France, 1682, at the age of 31

Mission: Christian education

Impact: During Fr de la Salle's lifetime, the Christian Brothers opened schools in Calais, Chartres, Rouen, Guise, and Rome. The institute would eventually number about 15,000 members operating schools throughout the world. The rule that Fr de la Salle composed and Benedict XII approved in 1725 has been adopted by many founders of teaching congregations.

Quote: "I will always look upon the work of my salvation, and the foundation and government of our community, as the work of God; hence I will abandon the care of both to Him, acting only through His orders;... I will often consider myself as an instrument which is of no use except in the hands of the workman. Hence I must await the orders of Providence before acting, and be careful to accomplish them when known."

Alphonsus Liguori

As the king of Naples' hunting-party tramped through the woods near Iliceto, they spied a large mansion screened behind some trees. The king inquired curiously who owned this fine "castle." One of the king's party reported that the house belonged to Alphonsus Liguori and his missionaries. Another added that these priests were rumored to be the recent inheritors of 60,000 ducats, an immense sum.

The king, a violent foe of religion, was surprised and angered that priests should be so wealthy and immediately ordered an investigation. The supposed wealth of the newly-founded Congregation of the Redeemer was fictitious, the house was so poor that it had been unable to sustain a novitiate. When the king realized the true situation of the Redemptorists, he canceled the investigation. Nevertheless, the incident worried Alphonsus.

Two years previously, the congregation had been approved by Pope Benedict XIV and had since enjoyed spectacular success in its missionary work among the people of Italy. However, the civil government had the power to bring all of the young congregation's activities to an end. If the Redemptorists were expelled from the kingdom, as the Jesuits had already been, it would mean the death of this new work of God.

The next year, Alphonsus obtained a royal decree sanctioning the houses already established at Iliceto, Pagani, Ciorani, and Caposele, but this decree was far from satisfactory in its details. Since these were the first and only houses of the congregation, Alphonsus seized every opportunity to attempt to win a more favorable approval. If the Redemptorists were to survive, they would have to obtain a more stable legal status.

However, complications soon arose. Two men, Canon Francis Maffei and Baron Nicholas Sarnelli, bore personal grievances against the congregation. Maffei, a local official of some importance, had been attempting for some time to control officials of both the local secular and ecclesiastical powers but had encountered opposition from the bishop. When Redemptorist priests, including Alphonsus himself, were asked to testify against him in court, the truthful evidence was so damaging that Maffei was banished from Iliceto. He never forgave the Redemptorists.

Sarnelli, meanwhile, wanted to repossess a vineyard that his brother, now dead, had once given to the congregation.

The two men launched their attacks. They accused the Redemptorists of violating the royal decree of 1752 and demanded that the congregation be suppressed.

The official prosecutor reported to the king on the charges of Maffei and Sarnelli. The report was worse than expected. Dwelling only briefly on the claims of Sarnelli, it concluded that the very existence of the Redemptorists in Naples was illegal.

The prosecutor charged that the Redemptorists were in fact the suppressed Society of Jesus in disguise. The prosecutor, having carefully studied the rule of the Redemptorists, announced that he found it to be practically identical to that of the Jesuits, with the same central organization and the same thinly-veiled ambition of infiltrating every position of power. Above all, their founder embraced the same system of morality as the Jesuits, a morality which the prosecutor termed "lax." There could be no doubt that Alphonsus was a Jesuit under a different name.

For this reason, concluded the prosecutor, the Redemptorists should be suppressed, their property sold, and the income divided among the members already in holy orders, while the novices were to be sent home.

Alphonsus had to call upon all his legal training and experience to avert the immediate danger. He was by now eighty-one years old, in poor health, partly blind, deaf, lame, and asthmatic. One by one he took up the accusations. When the day of the trial arrived, Maffei and Sarnelli consulted with the seven lawyers they had hired and decided not to risk their case. Instead, they asked for another adjournment, and again the case rested.

The next two years seemed to mark a turning point in the status of the congregation. It acquired friends at court, its missionary work continued, and its enemies remained quiet.

Negotiations at Naples

Alphonsus believed that the time was now ripe for complete royal approbation of his institute. Alphonsus wanted the king to approve the same rule Pope Benedict XIV had approved. Such an approval would render the congregation immune to civil attack and would ensure the final security of the congregation.

Alphonsus sought the opinion of Msgr Testa, the minister of religious affairs, who replied that the circumstances indeed looked favorable. As proof of his good will, Msgr Testa told Alphonsus that he would see to it that the matter received immediate attention from the king.

Alphonsus appointed Fr Majone, his long-time representative at the Neapolitan court, to take charge of the negotiations. Alphonsus instructed Fr Majone to prepare the manuscript of the rule asked for by Msgr Testa, and he gave strict orders not to compromise any essential point. But when Fr Majone began to confer with Msgr Testa, both saw at once that they would have to go farther in changing the rule than their commission empowered them.

Since Msgr Testa held office by favor of the king, he owed more loyalty to the king than to Alphonsus. He immediately began to make changes to customize the rule to suit the king's pleasure. He eliminated the vows of poverty, chastity, and obedience, the oath of perseverance in the congregation, the authority of the rector major, and the holding of chapters.

Fr Majone, wearied by long years of suffering as the congregation's agent in the litigation and trouble at Naples, allowed Msgr Testa to make the amendments. He believed the Redemptorists could accept the king's approval of a modified rule but continue living as they had lived before.

When rumors began to surface that radical changes were being made to the rule, various members of the congregation began to write letters of protest to Alphonsus.

Alphonsus responded to one of the letters, "I hear that some are thinking that I wish to make a new rule different from the old. How could anyone suspect this, since I have always been the most jealous of the rule? I have always governed the congregation according to the rule, and I will strive till my last breath to ensure that it shall not be changed even in its least part."

But to reassure himself, Alphonsus questioned Majone directly whether there would be any changes in the rule affecting the common life. Majone had gone too far to now retrace his steps, so he gave an evasive answer that relieved Alphonsus.

Meanwhile, after a month of negotiation at Naples, and as nervous tension built throughout the houses of the congregation, the amended rule was finally completed.

Majone now found himself faced with a difficult task. To present the amended rule to the king, he needed Alphonsus's signature. But Majone knew Alphonsus would never sign the manuscript if he was aware that it no longer included neither the three religious vows nor the internal structures that would guarantee the congregation's existence as a united whole. Nevertheless, he had to find a way to get his signature.

At this time, Alphonsus was practically blind and suffered severely from headaches. When Fr Majone brought him the document, Alphonsus took it and began to read.

The reading, however, with its marginal notes and interlinear corrections, tired Alphonsus and strained his weak eyes. He read far enough to realize that the first chapter had been hardly changed at all, but he had not yet reached the vital changes of the new version of the rule. He handed the document to his vicar general to read it for him. The vicar general had already been won over to Fr Majone's way of thinking and was convinced of the need to move forward. He read it hurriedly and, with a few general words of approval, handed it back to Alphonsus to sign.

Fr Majone returned to Naples with the signed document. When it came up for discussion at court, Msgr Testa had done his work well, and approval was granted almost immediately.

It was an empty victory for Fr Majone. He dreaded the job of announcing the approval, or even showing the document to

Alphonsus and the congregation, so he waited more than a month before sending it with another priest who was going to see Alphonsus.

Alphonsus was not well, so the fathers thought it unwise to trouble him when the letter arrived. Nevertheless, Alphonsus spoke enthusiastically of the anticipated approval and announced his plans for a general renewal of vows on Good Friday.

After dinner, the community gathered around the vicar general. Unable to restrain their curiosity any longer, they insisted that the vicar general open the letter in the name of Alphonsus. He broke the seal, and in a few moments all knew that the Redemptorists had been destroyed.

The next morning the fathers who had been present went to Alphonsus and, almost before revealing the contents of the letter, demanded an explanation. Alphonsus asked for a copy of the rule and burst into uncontrollable weeping when he read the revisions.

"I ought to be dragged through the streets," he said. "It was my duty as rector major to read the manuscript myself." Then turning to the vicar general he said, "Don Andrew Villani, I never thought I could be deceived in such a way by you. I have been betrayed."

Msgr Testa, on the other hand, was quite pleased with his work and sent an order that the revised rule be put into effect by March 1. "You," he wrote dictatorially to Alphonsus, "as founder and Superior General of the institute, will be good enough to tell all the subjects in my name that these statutes are to remain perpetually in force; no modifications will be permitted. The members of the institute, present or future, whether priests, students, or lay brothers, must submit themselves, each and every one of them, without opposition or contradiction. To achieve this you will communicate this mandate to all the local superiors, enjoining them to read it to their communities at the accustomed place and time of meeting. They should make a memorandum of the fact in their archives for future reference and notify me that they have executed this order."

But more was to come.

Crisis

Pope Pius VI, already indignant over the interference of secular authorities in religious matters, was led to believe that Alphonsus, weakened by old age, had consented to all the changes in the rule. To the Holy Father, it seemed as though Alphonsus had completely betrayed his principles in allowing a new rule in Naples, thus dividing the authority governing the congregation. In effect, this created a schism between the houses in Naples and those in the Papal States.

As Alphonsus was preparing to defend his case in Rome, the Sarnelli lawsuit resurfaced, reawakening the fears of complete suppression by the king. With Alphonsus distracted by the lawsuit, the pope proceeded to sign the decree excluding Alphonsus from his own congregation.

Those closest to Alphonsus could not bear to tell him what had happened. They waited until the next morning when Alphonsus was preparing for Mass.

He broke into tears when he heard the pope's decree and then began to blame himself for the ruin of the congregation. After a while, he became calm: "I want only what God wants. His grace is sufficient for me. The pope will have it so. God be praised." Then he continued his preparation for Mass.

During the day, however, all the bitterness of the catastrophe descended upon him. He had constant recourse to prayer to the Blessed Virgin Mary, to whom he had always had a special devotion, but it was only after several hours that the storm subsided and he was able to speak calmly of what had happened. "The pope has thought it to be good. God be praised. The will of the pope is the will of God."

Alphonsus was almost eighty-six years old when he was cut off from the congregation. It was the end of his external activities. Despite the interior trials and afflictions of these years, his firm belief in Divine Providence never wavered: he prophesied that after his death the congregation would spread its wings far and wide. He prepared for death with the same spirit of humility and submission to God's will.

Years later, when news of his imminent death spread, large numbers of every rank and station gathered at the monastery to see for the last time the man whom all revered as a saint. He died on August 1, 1787.

At Rome it was decided to introduce the cause of his canonization, but the objection was immediately raised that Alphonsus had abandoned a rule approved by the Church. Pius VI, remembering the controversy all too well, appointed three cardinals to examine the whole question and gave them the mandate to settle the question definitively.

After an investigation, the cardinals unanimously decided that the affair of the rule was in no way a blot on his conscience. Rather, they judged, it was something which God had permitted in order to purify him through the great suffering it caused.

The same pope who had expelled him from his congregation was the pope who beatified him. Alphonsus Liguori was eventually canonized on May 26, 1839. By the time of his canonization his congregation had opened houses in various countries in Europe and America. The first foundation in Portugal was made in 1826, in Belgium in 1831, in America in 1832, and in Holland in 1836. When Alphonsus was hailed as a saint, his congregation had thirty-one houses, nine of them beyond Italy. His congregation had indeed spread its wings far and wide.

Alphonsus Liguori

Lifetime: Born in 1696, died in 1787 at the age of 90

Order: Redemptorists

Founded: Scala, Italy, 1732, at the age of 36

Mission: Preaching through the use of retreats, missions, and novenas

Impact: Liguori founded both the Redemptorists and the Redemptoristine nuns; both have spread worldwide. His prolific theological and mystical writings enjoy considerable influence even today.

Quote: "Persecutions are to the works of God what the frosts of winter are to plants. Far from destroying them, they allow them to strike their roots deeper in soil and make them more full of life. What really injures religious orders and brings the plant to decay like a worm gnawing at the root are voluntary sins and shortcomings. So let us put an end to these imperfections, let us correct ourselves, and God will protect us. The more violently persecution rages, the more closely must we become attached to Jesus Christ."

Edmund Rice

Edmund was trying to figure out what he would do with his life. Years before, he had become an apprentice in a well-established shipping company owned by his uncle. When Edmund was twenty-four, his uncle had signed the thriving company over to him. At that time, he had fallen in love with a beautiful young woman, the daughter of a leather merchant. Their subsequent marriage was a short one, however. Four years later, his young wife was killed by falling from a horse on a hunting trip.

The wealthy young Edmund was troubled. Convinced that something more was wanted of him, he came up with a plan to travel to Rome and visit the tombs of the martyrs and the catacombs of the early Christians. Upon his return to Ireland, he would embrace a solitary life by becoming a lay Augustinian brother.

When he mentioned the idea to a woman he knew in Waterford, she asked him, "Would you not be better off doing something for poor boys similar to what the Presentation nuns are doing in Cork for poor girls?"

The only schools offering free education in Ireland at that time were financed by English sources who wanted to destroy the Catholic faith in Ireland. Edmund's own bishop had written a pastoral letter condemning these schools and reprimanding Catholic parents who risked their children's faith by sending them to such schools. It was a difficult situation for poor people: their only hope for their children's education lay in these free schools, but at the cost of their children's faith.

Edmund, who sympathized with their plight, was determined to allay the situation. He presented the bishop of Ossory with a proposal which was very well-received. In 1796 he sent an outline of his idea to Pope Pius VI, who encouraged Edmund to proceed with his plan.

Not long afterwards, a young woman looking for work knocked at the rectory of St John's parish in Waterford. She had been educated by the Presentation nuns in Cork, and Fr John Power, the pastor, was so impressed by her level of education that he asked the nuns to establish a convent in Waterford.

He was told that no one was immediately available. However, if volunteers came forward, they could be trained in Cork and then sent back to Waterford to establish a foundation there. Two of Fr Power's relatives did just that. Upon completing their novitiate and professing their vows, they arrived in Waterford and opened a temporary school in September of 1798.

Edmund, a close friend of Fr Power, acquired land for the sisters on which a permanent convent adjacent to the school was to be erected. He did all he could to help build the convent.

His involvement in this project increased Edmund's interest in the apostolate of Catholic education, and he at last made his decision. Selling his business, he set to work on the creation of his own school. After his wife's death he had inherited a large stable in the New Street area of Waterford which he now converted into a two-story school building. He began with six students.

At this time Edmund's brother, Fr John Rice, sent to him two men eager to consecrate their lives to God. They were interested in teaching and hoped to join the religious congregation they knew Edmund wanted to found.

The three of them lived in the upper level above the stables and began to follow a regular discipline of prayer, work, and recreation. Almost immediately the classrooms filled. Demand was so great that they soon had to open an additional school nearby.

Their schools quickly spread across Ireland, and on September 5, 1820, the Irish Christian Brothers were recognized by Pope Pius VII. The brothers rejoiced, but there was one particular clause in the papal brief which was to cause Edmund much grief. Article 5 stated that the brothers should teach gratis, accepting neither compensation nor reward from the parents; Edmund thought this too restrictive.

An Autocrat

He made his first request to Rome to open fee-paying schools in January of 1823. The Holy See referred the matter to the Bishop of Waterford, Patrick Kelly, who replied, "I am decidedly of the opinion that the petition should not be granted. I see no reason for such an application, since it does not seem right in this wretched country."

Moreover, many of the brothers opposed the idea of fee-paying schools. They believed that the Irish Christian Brothers had one reason for existence: the free education of the poor. They argued that fee-paying schools contradicted the spirit and rule of the congregation, and they feared that the fee-paying schools would get all the best teachers at the expense of the free ones. Some members of the congregation grumbled, "He started the congregation for the poor; that's why we joined. Now he is changing his mind."

Yet in spite of all this, Edmund remained steadfast, for he was convinced that there was a need for fee-paying schools. As a result, Edmund's leadership became increasingly criticized as autocratic. Some demanded more democracy; many others pushed for a second chapter in order to make the necessary changes.

Letters such as the following were circulated, "Edmund is in a very pitiable condition. His mind is so disordered that he is completely incapable of applying himself to the business of the Institute.... Edmund is inclined to set himself against the view of his two Assistants in all matters concerning the welfare of the Institute. Very often he tells them that he will not listen to any remonstrance of theirs and that he is not obliged to follow their advice unless it agrees with his own opinions. His mind has been thus deranged for a long time. It seems to me that his illness will be of long duration.... The brothers wish to settle several matters regarding the nature and stability of the Institute; they are determined to assemble."

The push for a new chapter increased until Edmund finally yielded. During the first session it was proposed that Edmund be restricted from making propositions or recommending amendments on the grounds that he would exercise too great an influence. When he heard this, he tendered his resignation as Superior General. Kneeling before the brothers, Edmund read a short statement of resignation and then left the room.

The brothers were shocked by this unexpected development. They quickly rejected his resignation and insisted that he preside over the remainder of the chapter, but it remained an intensely unhappy time for him.

At the age of seventy-six, Edmund decided his health would no longer permit him to deal with the administrative demands of the congregation. He convoked another chapter, where he announced his retirement. By a vote of nine to eight, the chapter elected Br Michael Riordan, a long time opponent of Edmund on the issue of fee-paying schools, to serve for life as Superior General.

Three years later, at the start of the next chapter, Edmund went to the assembly room thinking that as ex-Superior General he was entitled to attend. He was received coldly and was asked to withdraw while they discussed the question of his admission. It was decided that the founder could not take part in the chapter of his own congregation, not even as an observer.

Vindicated

After retirement, Edmund faded into the background. He kept himself informed about school affairs, but he himself did not dare to intrude. Although he was concerned about the new policies being followed and the discord which they caused, he did not challenge the authority of the Superior General.

But God has His way.

Edmund's friend, Archbishop Murray of Dublin, was also concerned about the great number of children in his diocese who were either attending the English schools or none at all. Working tirelessly, he opened two hundred schools in forty-eight parishes during his life.

The Irish Christian Brothers played a crucial part in this development, and Archbishop Murray was eager to help them in every possible way. He wanted as many schools as he could get, and it mattered little to him if they were free or not. The inability of Edmund's institute to operate fee-paying schools was becoming an obstacle to his work, so he took steps to have this impediment removed.

Several senior Irish Christian Brothers wrote Rome describing the state of their institutions: of the eighteen houses they had founded, only five had funds to cover maintenance expenses. While the English government lavished money on their public schools, the brothers were not infrequently forced to go begging from door to door in order to keep their own schools open. The only other means of raising funds was the annual charity sermons. However, if the local bishop or pastor did not like the brothers, these were prohibited.

The situation is described in a letter: "We find from experience how galling it is when after spending five days in our schools we must sally forth on the sixth day to beg from house to house for the pennies and half-pennies to support us for the ensuing week."

There were indeed thousands of parents who could not afford to pay anything for their children's education; but there were other parents who were able to pay, and others still who could at least contribute something.

In 1873, the Holy See issued a brief granting the Irish Christian Brothers permission to establish fee-paying schools wherever they wished. Edmund's far-sighted policy was vindicated in its entirety.

Edmund Rice

Lifetime: Born in 1762, died in 1844 at the age of 82

Order: Irish Christian Brothers

Founded: Waterford, Ireland, 1802, at the age of 40

Mission: Christian education

Impact: At Edmund Rice's retirement, the congregation had 22 houses in Ireland and England. It has now spread throughout the English-speaking world and South America. The Presentation Brothers also recognize him as their founder. He was beatified in 1996.

Quote: "As worldly people love and seek with great diligence honor, fame, and high reputation, so they who are spiritual and who seriously follow Christ love and ardently desire the opposite; insomuch that, could it be done without sin, they would willingly suffer contumely, false testimony, and injuries and desire to be esteemed as fools (giving no occasion thereto) in order to resemble Jesus Christ, who has given the example, and who is the way, the truth, and the life that leads to glory."

Therese Couderc

It was the spring of 1837, and religious life was again flourishing in France after the bloody and terrifying days of the Revolution. The Sisters of the Cenacle, the congregation of nuns which Mother Therese Couderc had founded, was nine years old. Therese had taken her inspiration for the congregation's name and apostolate from the time which the Blessed Virgin spent with the apostles in the upper room, or cenacle, awaiting the coming of the Holy Spirit.

The sisters' work of giving retreats was thriving and the community continued to grow, especially under the guidance of Jesuit priests who had been close to the congregation from the beginning. Soon it became necessary for the sisters to build a new convent and chapel. The work began well, but suddenly the funding for this new project evaporated. The congregation was saddled with enormous debts and little hope to pay them.

Rumors began to circulate. "They say that Therese is incompetent and has no business ability whatsoever. How can we count on her to raise funds for the congregation if she is going to fail like this? And her health is reported to be failing badly; perhaps she is no longer capable of governing. It is possible that she has mental problems." The bishop of Viviers lost his trust in her, reinforcing Mother Therese's own humble but mistaken conviction that she was to blame for the debacle. At last, she resigned her office of superior. She was thirty-three years old, having guided her sisters for the first ten years of the congregation's existence.

The Trials Begin

Her successor, chosen by the Jesuit provincial, was Mademoiselle Gallet, a wealthy widow only 20 years old, who had been a novice for only 15 days. When she died later that year, she left her fortune to the congregation. However, her relatives contested her will, and the Cenacle's financial situation was once more thrown into disarray. The bishop of Viviers named Countess de la Villeurnoy the new superior general. Soon, she even began to call herself "mother founder."

Although the Countess had good intentions, she lacked not only Mother Therese's vision, but also a solid conception of religious life. She relaxed Mother Therese's rule of strict observance of silence and poverty, which had been at the heart of the congregation's spirituality.

Countess de la Villeurnoy was uncomfortable with evangelical poverty. She even went so far as to place the community still further in debt by borrowing money to purchase fine furnishings for the house.

Mother Therese's greatest suffering in all of this was to see her beloved community so roughly handled. The laity were scandalized, the community suffered, and rumors of this state of affairs reached Fr François Renault, the local provincial of the Jesuits. When the provincial visited the convent, he summoned Mother Therese.

"It seems that no one can govern this congregation," he began. "You yourself resigned your office in disgrace, and this Countess has led you all to the brink of disaster. Now it falls to me to pick up the pieces. Tell me: should I assign a new superior? Would it help this congregation function better?"

Mother Therese remained silent for a moment. "Fr Renault," she said carefully, "You know that I am a professed religious, and that I have taken a vow of obedience to my superiors for life. To me, that obedience means that I must respect every action of my superiors, whether it appeals to me or not. God has placed Mother de la Villeurnoy in a position of authority over me; you seek testimony which I cannot give nor do I wish to give."

The provincial was dumbfounded. "But this woman calls herself the founder! She has stolen the respect that is rightfully yours!" he burst out.

"Perhaps," Mother Therese said quietly. "But more important than any title is the vow which I have made to my Creator and Redeemer."

Nevertheless, the provincial did not need her testimony; there was more than enough evidence against the Countess. After causing eleven months of havoc, the Countess was removed from office.

Mother Contenet, her replacement, did much good for the congregation. Eager to attract members of the higher social classes for the congregation, she expelled ten of the original twelve members of the congregation. Convinced of the ineptitude of the true founder, she did everything in her power to keep Mother Therese away from the other sisters. Therese was exiled from her chosen work of giving retreats to spend thirteen years at the most difficult manual labor in the congregation, working in the gardens and the cellar. Conditions were so poor that her eyesight was permanently impaired. Her food was only the worst of the vegetables and the unwanted remnants of black bread which the gardener threw alongside the convent wall.

Mother Therese dropped into increasing obscurity. "After all," she reflected, "the religious life is a sufficiently great grace even though one purchase it at the price of the most difficult of sacrifices." Despite the great mortification of her state, she told the young religious that "We should never allow even one thought of sadness to enter the soul. Have we not within us Him who is the joy of Heaven!"

Mother Therese's exile ended with the death of Mother Contenet in 1852, but dissension and instability once more returned to the Cenacle. Mother Anaïs was elected the new superior general, but left the congregation three years later. Not until 1856 did Therese return to an active role in the congregation.

During a time of crisis, Mother Therese was sent briefly to serve as temporary superior of the convent in Paris and then at Tournon, where her governance was remembered for its firmness but genuine goodness. Again, however, she disappeared into the background.

One day, while visiting one of the convents of the Religious of the Cenacle, Cardinal Lavigerie noticed Mother Therese praying in the chapel. He turned to the superior of the house and asked, "Anyone can see how holy the face of this sister is. What is her name?"

"Sister Therese Couderc," was the reply.

"She seems such a saint," he mused. "What is her place in the history of the congregation?"

The superior was embarrassed. "Well, she was in charge of the gardens for many years, and she was sent to be a temporary superior at two houses in the 1850's. Now she just mostly prays in the chapel, and we let her alone."

Cardinal Lavigerie looked at her sharply. "She has been left out, hasn't she?" The superior said nothing.

Her reputation had been by now so thoroughly maligned by her superiors that even her status as founder had been completely forgotten. Her work as founder had been, above all, her prayers, penances, and humiliation. It was only towards the end of her life, when bishop of Viviers launched an inquiry into the circumstances of the foundation, that Mother Therese Couderc was finally recognized as the founder of the Sisters of the Cenacle.

Therese Couderc

Lifetime: Born in 1805, died in 1885 at the age of 80

Order: Society of Our Lady of the Retreat in the Cenacle
(Sisters of the Cenacle)

Founded: La Louvesc, France, 1828, at the age of 23

Mission: Catechesis and retreats for lay women

Impact: The Sisters of the Cenacle experienced their most dramatic growth after the death of their founder; by 1960, the congregation could count 71 houses and 1,500 members worldwide.

Quote: "I ask of God that we shall never do anything to show off; but that we should on the contrary do our good in the background, and that we should always look upon ourselves as the least of the Church's little ones."

Anthony Mary Claret

The courier made his way up the center aisle of the packed church in Santiago, Cuba. He approached the pulpit, where Anthony Mary Claret was giving one of his customary impassioned sermons. The archbishop paused for a moment and peered down at the unexpected visitor, who handed up a large sealed envelope and departed in silence.

The archbishop had not brought his reading glasses, so he did not open the envelope until he returned to his residence. As he walked in the door, he asked one of his canons to read him the message. It was surprising news from the commandant of Santiago: "It is the queen's pleasure that you leave immediately for Madrid. Tomorrow I shall forward the formal order and place a ship at your disposal."

Upon his arrival in Spain, he received the news that he was to be the queen's confessor, a highly influential position at the Spanish court. The never-ending conflict between the pressures of office and the dictates of her conscience had exhausted her, and she was convinced that no one in Spain could fill the post of court confessor better than Anthony Claret.

As far as Claret was concerned, nothing could have repelled him more: he not only hated having to abandon all his work, but he also loathed politics. Furthermore, he could not help wondering if he was not becoming a pawn in the desperate game the enemies of the Church were waging for political control of Spain.

All Anthony Claret really wanted was to return to the congregation he had founded several years before. The Missionary Sons of the Immaculate Heart of Mary, later known as the Claretians, were dedicated to preaching and catechizing. They also operated a small publishing company which he had begun and for which he wrote many of the first pieces. The discipline and spirit of the congregation focused on poverty, avoiding honors, and accepting calumnies, and loving one's enemy. At the heart of their spirituality was the search for perfection through prayer and meditation.

Once he had established the publishing company, Claret's next step was to devote himself entirely to expanding the congregation. But less than a month after foundation, he was appointed Archbishop of Santiago. He was thunderstruck. All his plans would have to be dropped. Reluctantly, he left behind his small, struggling community.

Now, after six years of tireless work to rebuild the Church in Cuba, he was again asked to take yet another step further away from his desire to consolidate his order. He told the queen he was not ready to make a decision, and he consulted the papal nuncio about taking the position of court confessor. "For the good of Spain," was the answer, "it is better for you to accept." He accepted the post and named Fr Jose Xifre the superior general of the congregation.

Claret wrote to a friend, "You have no idea of the grief such a nomination occasions in my heart. It ruins my apostolic plans. Seeing the scarcity of preachers in the Spanish territory, the great desire of the people to hear the Divine Word, and the many requests I receive to go preach the gospel throughout Spain, I wanted to gather and train a number of companions, to accomplish with others what I could not do alone."

The Storm Breaks

Storm clouds were gathering on the political horizon. The queen's enemies plotted to overthrow the government, but they realized that a direct attack would be futile. They first had to topple the queen's strongest moral support, one of the most revered men in Spain: Anthony Claret stood in their way.

On October 15, 1859, a man entered the church where Claret was preaching, intent on murdering the queen's confessor. The secret society to which the man belonged had given him forty days to "eliminate" Claret, and the assassin's time was running out. If he failed, he would be killed, just as he himself had killed other unsuccessful assassins.

But once inside the church, an unaccountable change of heart overcame him, and he found himself weeping at the very feet of the man he was going to kill. Claret embraced and forgave his would-be assassin, and the man set off to hide from the society.

Not long after this, a well-dressed man appeared at Montserrat, urgently requesting to see Claret. He was informed that His Excellency would doubtless see him at the close of the sermon he was delivering in the hospital church. The stranger grew tired of waiting and decided that he might as well go in to hear the last sermon Claret would ever preach.

As he slipped into the back of the church, he heard the conclusion of the sermon: "If the enthusiasm with which I speak of the glories of my most holy Mother Mary surprises you, know it could hardly be less, inasmuch as all my life long she has been my Protectress, and even at this instant she is freeing me from a greater danger that threatens me."

After Mass, the man approached Claret penitently, holding out the dagger with which he had intended to end the priest's life. This man, too, had to flee the secret society's wrath, and Claret supplied him with a disguise, some money, and a passport.

Attacks from the Press

Failing to eliminate Claret through violence, the queen's enemies adopted alternative measures. They planned to discredit and humiliate Claret before the eyes of his tremendous following. The press launched the first accusations, alleging that Claret was involved in an improper relationship with the queen. Moreover, they claimed that he attracted vast audiences of listeners with graphic descriptions in his sermons of the most abominable sins.

Then an unauthorized edition of his latest book, "The Golden Key," was published with pornographic illustrations. Simultaneously, two slanderous new biographies of Claret appeared on the market. The clergy of Madrid was shocked.

Although the political climate was rapidly decaying, the queen remained unaware of the looming disaster. "The Lord is angry with this nation," Claret kept warning. "He has told me a great revolution will fall upon Spain. The queen will be dethroned, a republic declared, and many innocent people will suffer."

When the revolution came in the form of a military coup, the queen was exiled from Spain. In the purges that followed, the upstart government murdered a number of Claretians. Claret escaped with the royal family to the relative safety of Paris, while his congregation established themselves at Prades, just across the border from Spain.

Later, some jewels were found missing from the Escorial near

Madrid, and Claret was "discovered" to have stolen them. Spanish newspaper editorials demanded his extradition from France, and he was depicted in cartoons fleeing from Spain burdened with an expensive monstrance.

The Final Journeys

Claret's one consolation in the course of his exile was his active participation in the First Vatican Council. As the debates raged over the doctrine of papal infallibility, Claret held his tongue. But as he listened to one particularly misleading and deceptive argument, he became so outraged that he suffered a stroke. Despite the urgings of friends, he remained at the council, delivering a passionate confession of faith in the infallibility of the pope. The council voted in his favor.

Though his heart was consoled, his body was quickly deteriorating. News of his physical state soon reached the superior general, Fr Xifre, who immediately left for Rome. Upon his arrival, he was overwhelmed by how much his founder's health had declined. Yet, he feared bringing Claret back home to Prades, so close to Spain and so far from the protecting influence of the royal family in Paris. But there was no other option. "I am taking you back to Prades, no matter what the French authorities say," he resolutely told his founder.

Back in Padres, it no longer seemed necessary to conceal

Claret's presence at Prades. So when he was invited to speak at the neighboring seminary of Fontfroide, he did so in his native Catalan, a language very similar to French. It was a mistake.

Some time later, Fr Xifre received a letter containing the worst possible news. The Spanish consul at Perpignan had received word that Claret had been located at Prades and had solicited authorization for his arrest. On August 5, it became known that a warrant authorizing his arrest had been signed. It was a final act of malice on the part of his persecutors. To avoid this, he would have to go into hiding at once.

The superior of the seminary at Fontfroide suggested to Fr Xifre, "Bring him here to the monastery; we have prepared a room for him." The local bishop approved the plan, and at daybreak, Anthony Claret was carried to the monastery by his Claretians. It proved to be his last journey. Upon his arrival, Anthony told the monks, "All my life I have looked forward to ending my days in a monastery." There he died on the morning of October 24, 1870.

Anthony Mary Claret

Lifetime: Born in 1807, died in 1870 at the age of 63

Order: Missionary Sons of the Immaculate Heart of Mary (Claretians)

Founded: Vich, Spain, 1848, at the age of 42

Mission: Preaching by means of retreats, missions, and the printed press

Impact: By the time of Anthony Claret's canonization, there were 4000 Claretians living in 240 religious houses in 24 countries.

Quote: "I can see what they say of me. I can only comment that it is a reminder of the patrimony left us by Christ. This is the pay the world accords us. We do well to recall the words of Isaiah, 'Your strength is in silence and hope.' Blessed be You, my God. Give Your holy blessing to all who persecute and calumniate me. Give them, Lord, prosperity—spiritual, corporal, temporal, eternal. And to me give humility, gentleness, patience, and conformity to Your holy Will, that I may suffer in silence and love the pain, persecution, and calumny that You permit to descend upon me."

Jeanne Jugan

In 1837 Jeanne Jugan and two companions decided to move into a two-room apartment on Center Street and lead a life of prayer and dedication to God. Jeanne had always been sensitive to the things of God, and she saw Him reflected in the numberless faces of the poor of France.

One day she encountered Anne Chauvin, a blind old widow with no one to look after her, and decided to bring her home. Since the apartment was on the second floor, Jeanne had to physically carry her up the narrow stairs. Jeanne gave her bed to Anne and moved into the loft.

Before long she took in another old woman, and Jeanne and her two companions had to work to support and feed themselves and two others. They would often stay up late at night mending and washing clothes and get up early each morning to care for the women in their charge.

Often on Sundays the three of them would go for a walk

together along the seashore, stopping at a favorite cleft in the rocks to talk about God, their lives, and their plans for the future.

They would also discuss these matters with a young priest who had recently arrived to the parish. Fr le Pailleur was immediately interested in the work and gave it his full approval. A very capable, sometimes daring, and often ingenious man, he too had aspirations to help the poor; he felt compelled to support this work which held so much promise.

Visiting them at their home, he met with the three of them, and together they resolved to create a charitable association. Jeanne was delighted with the help promised by this young priest who approved of their mad plan. In very little time they were taking in more and more people, urged on by the desire to share the poverty and distress of those whom they sought to help and to alleviate their plight as much as possible.

Begging

Less than three years after this foundation, Jeanne and her companions moved down the street into their first house. Their new home was spacious, built around a courtyard large enough to make a proper dormitory. That same day six more women joined the group; many more would soon follow.

To support this growth, Jeanne devoted herself to begging. One young visitor to the new house wrote, "I saw Jeanne Jugan. She greeted me and my grandmother with a kind smile as she was preparing to go out collecting. Over her arm she put her basket, already such a well-known sight all over town. The old women called her Sister Jeanne. 'Sister Jeanne,' they would say, 'do our job properly for us. Collect for us.' Jeanne would lean over them and listen to a few more whispered instructions; she smiled at them. She left them promptly, for she did things quickly, yet she never gave the impression of hurrying or being hurried."

One day she rang the doorbell of a rich man notorious for his miserliness and persuaded him to donate a sizable gift. The next day she called again; at this he became very angry. She simply smiled and said, "Sir, my poor were hungry yesterday, they are hungry again today, and tomorrow they will be hungry too." The man became a regular benefactor of Jeanne's works.

On another occasion Jeanne went to beg from a local ship owner, a fiery man given to violent fits of passion. Jeanne was the only person who knew how to manage his explosive temper. One time he was overseeing the unloading of one of his ships. Among the cargo were some small but enormously valuable bags filled with gold ingots. As the cargo was being unloaded one of these bags dropped into the water, provoking one of the man's characteristic eruptions. Just at this moment Jeanne came along seeking a donation from him. While still some distance away, she saw that something was wrong and approached to see if she could help. He immediately launched into a tirade about what had happened.

Promising to pray for the recovery of the lost money, Jeanne continued on her way.

The bag was eventually recovered, and when Jeanne passed by a short time later she remarked, "I told you God would recover your money."

The man looked almost sheepish for a moment, but he quickly regained his customary brusque demeanor. "Here," he growled. "Take the bag. This is for your little old folks."

Recognition

Each year the prestigious Montyon Award was presented by the French Academy to a poor French man or woman who performed outstanding public service. Some of Jeanne's friends decided to submit her name as a candidate for the award. They prepared a brief memorial and presented it to the Academy for consideration. Several months later her friends were informed that Jeanne Jugan had been awarded the first prize, a total of three thousand francs. The money arrived just in time to pay for the new roof and some furniture which she had bought.

Jeanne soon realized she could use this award to advertise her work to the civil authorities. As one unexpected result of this publicity, she received a large gold medal as an award from the local Masonic Lodge. She promptly had it melted down and used the gold for a chalice.

The Deception

The little group continued to grow, and on December 8, 1842, the first "sisters" took a vow of obedience, thus establishing the Little Sisters of the Poor. In their first election, Jeanne Jugan was chosen as Mother Superior. However, two weeks later Fr le Pailleur called a surprise meeting. He nullified the election and named the timid twenty-three year old Marie Jamet in Jeanne's place.

Eight years later, Fr le Pailleur drafted the definitive constitution of the institute with the help of another priest who had assisted Jeanne from the beginning. In the document, Fr le Pailleur carefully assured that the office of Fr Superior General be given absolute authority over the congregation. The next year, the constitution was approved, and the Little Sisters of the Poor became a recognized congregation within the Church. The bishop was present when twenty-four postulants received their uniform and seventeen novices professed vows.

Fr le Pailleur had every reason to be satisfied. He had now secured the office of Fr Superior General of the congregation, and consequently he had full authority. At this point, he made an important decision.

Calling Jeanne into his office, he told her she was to retire to the mother house. He ordered her to cut off all connection with her benefactors and friends and to no longer go out begging. She was to devote herself entirely to prayer and overseeing the manual work of the postulants. In everything, Jeanne obeyed with complete submission.

Gradually, Fr le Pailleur began to insinuate that he had always been the driving force behind the congregation. The story gradually spread that he had begun this work by recruiting two other sisters before encountering Jeanne Jugan. When he saw her talent for fundraising, he immediately set her to work begging for the sisters and the elderly in their charge. To bolster this story, he placed a plaque outside their first home which read, "Here Fr le Pailleur, founder of the Congregation of the Little Sisters of the Poor, began his work by helping a poor blind woman. He entrusted her to his two spiritual daughters to take her into the attic of this house where Jeanne Jugan was living. To their number, the founder soon added Jeanne Jugan, who discharged her duty of collecting with admirable devotion."

As the Little Sisters continued to grow and spread across the French countryside, journalists began to report this story, lending it still more credibility. Even the new novices were taught that Fr le Pailleur was the founder of the congregation. For all those who had known Jeanne in the early years, this caused great confusion.

He became ever more inflated with pride, demanding the most exaggerated signs of respect and flattery from the sisters; if they met him going for a walk they had to kiss his feet and ask for his blessing. Even his admirers became disquieted by the spectacle.

Out of obedience, Jeanne did nothing to dispel these false-hoods. Some postulants who had heard that Jeanne was the founder kept trying to get the whole story from her. Knowing the version of the story taught in the novitiate, Jeanne would say evasively, "They'll tell you all about that in the novitiate." Then she would add, "Later, you'll know all about that."

On one occasion, Jeanne, with her head in her hands, groaned, "They have stolen my work from me!" She later repeated these words jokingly to Fr le Pailleur, adding, "But I willingly give it to you."

"I Am Not the First Little Sister"

As the years went by, the witnesses began to pass away one by one. Eventually Jeanne herself died, twenty-seven years after being confined to the mother house. Rumors of the injustice ultimately reached Rome, where they raised some eyebrows. An apostolic inquiry was begun.

In 1890, Fr le Pailleur was summoned to Rome, eleven years after Jeanne Jugan had passed away. He spent his last five years in a convent, relieved of his office as Fr Superior General.

The new chaplain at the mother house began to conduct an historical investigation into the origins of the congregation. He interviewed the founding sisters who were still alive and began to reconstruct the true story of the foundation. The most important document of the inquiry was the memorial for the Academy Award, written in Fr le Pailleur's handwriting, which named Jeanne Jugan as the founder.

Marie Jamet, the Mother Superior whom Fr le Pailleur had named to replace Jeanne, lived to see the conclusion. "I am not the first Little Sister, nor the founder of the work," she testified. "Jeanne Jugan was the first one and the founder of the Little Sisters of the Poor." On her death bed she said, "I am not the first one but I was told to act as though I were."

From that point on, Jeanne Jugan would be called "Founder of the Little Sisters of the Poor." From God's point of view, those twenty-seven years of silent faith had proven to be the most fruitful of her life.

Jeanne Jugan

Lifetime: Born in 1792, died in 1879 at the age of 86

Order: Little Sisters of the Poor

Founded: Saint-Servan, France, 1842, at the age of 50

Mission: Care for the elderly

Impact: By the time of Jeanne's death, there were 2400 Little Sisters of the Poor in 10 different countries.

Quote: "Go and find him when your patience and strength run out and you feel alone and helpless. Jesus is waiting for you in the chapel. Say to him, 'Jesus, You know exactly what is going on. You are all I have, and You know all things. Come to my help.' And then go, and don't worry about how you are going to manage. That you have told God about it is enough. He has a good memory."

Don Bosco

Archbishop Gastaldi had been one of Don Bosco's most trusted friends for thirty-one years. But he had for some time held serious reservations about the methods which Don Bosco and his Salesians employed. After six months in his new Archdiocese of Turin, the center of Salesian activity, his attitude toward the newly-founded congregation was growing worse, as his advisors pointed out how Don Bosco ignored the archdiocese.

"Why is Don Bosco setting up his seminary against ours? Do his schools conform to the diocesan guidelines? One privilege after another! He must have a direct line to the Vatican, because he certainly does not come to us."

In 1874 Don Bosco began an association for late vocations and wanted to publish a booklet explaining the purposes of the association, but was denied an imprimatur by the Archdiocese of Turin. He had to ask his good friend, the bishop of Fossano, for an imprimatur. On the advice of Rome, he opened his first seminary for late vocations not in Turin but near Genoa.

Don Bosco frequently invited Archbishop Gastaldi to preside at Mass during one of the Salesian solemnities, but every invitation was met with a refusal. He asked him to give his boys Confirmation, for the pupils of the house had not had the opportunity to receive the sacrament for nearly four years. Again, the request was denied.

In 1879, the Bruno Press of Turin published pamphlets attacking the Archbishop. One accused him of doctrinal errors and the other criticized him for his unjust treatment of Don Bosco. Immediately, Don Bosco fell under suspicion of being the author. The indignant archbishop insisted that Don Bosco make a declaration formally condemning the pamphlets. Instead, he wrote a letter disapproving the disrespectful tone of the pamphlets, but he did not censure their content. Consequently, he continued to be regarded as the inspiration for the pamphlets, if not the actual author.

"Does it really matter if he literally wrote it? Does anyone doubt that he is thinking such things as well? He has not denied the content, has he? Where there's smoke, there's fire. Don Bosco is systematically opposing the archbishop. He wants to set himself above his authority and is carrying on a secret campaign against him."

At last, when a suit was brought against him in the Roman Court, Don Bosco for the first time felt he had to speak out. He wrote a long, detailed statement to the Congregation of Religious affirming that neither he nor any member of the congregation had taken any part in composing or editing the pamphlets. However, he found himself unable to condemn their content, for much of it was true.

When Pope Leo XIII read the statement, he was deeply moved; the strength of the case and its sincerity stirred him to the heart, so he had the case brought before him. He dictated a proposal for an agreement designed to put an end to the dispute.

Pope Leo sent the text to the Prefect of the Congregation, Cardinal Nina, who read the first article: "On receiving these instructions Don Bosco shall write a letter to Archbishop Gastaldi expressing his regret that, during these last few years, incidents should have affected their relationship and offended the archbishop. If the archbishop thought that he or any member of his institute were to blame, Don Bosco shall beg his pardon and ask him to forget the past."

"This clause seems unjust," said the Cardinal.

"I know what I am doing," replied Leo.

When the proposal was read to a gathering of Salesian superiors, they reacted as Cardinal Nina had. "We cannot accept it, Don Bosco," they declared. "Think of us; think of the future generations of Salesians and what history will say. You have to defend yourself!"

"And you, Cagliero, what do you think?" asked Don Bosco,

turning to the only one who had said nothing.

"I think it is just; the pope knows Don Bosco's virtue and love of peace, and he must hope to settle the matter once and for all by placing the burden unjustly upon the shoulders of the innocent."

Don Bosco heeded this advice and faithfully carried out the instructions contained in the papal document.

Even so, the conflicts between Archbishop Gastaldi and the founder continued, and in private the pope deplored that Don Bosco should encounter opposition from the very person from whom he had a right to expect support.

Once, while still friends with Don Bosco, Archbishop Gastaldi had given him the following advice: "Whenever you meet with human opposition, do not be alarmed nor allow any of your sons to display any resentment. Be sure that patience, prayers, and humility before God and men will be the best way to overcome your obstacles. All the holy founders have acted in this way."

The Search

As difficult as the conflict with Archbishop Gastaldi was for Don Bosco, it was by no means his only problem. During this turbulent time of Italian unification, opposition to the Papal States ran high. Because of Don Bosco's connections with the Holy See, the government suspected that he was opposed to a united Italy.

Wild speculations began to circulate.

"Why is he working with these boys? What does he want? He must be organizing a secret army to fight for the pope. The boys are being taught reactionary principles. He is hiding arms and ammunition in the seminary."

Moreover, their suspicions seemed to be confirmed when they saw high walls being built around the seminary. Louis Farini, Minister of the Interior, ordered the seminary to be searched for anything of an incriminating nature, such as arms, documents, or large sums of money.

One afternoon, a band of police officers came to the seminary telling Don Bosco they had orders to conduct a search.

"Please show me your search warrant," he said. The police had not brought it with them. Their presence normally caused so much alarm that most people never thought to ask for it.

"Otherwise," he continued, "I shall not be able to let you enter these premises."

"Are you going to stop us?" retorted one of the officers.

"Surely," said Don Bosco, "you would not dare to use force. I am only a private citizen, but under the Constitution my home is inviolable. As long as you give me no search warrant, I have my rights."

Left with no other option, they hastened to the Ministry to fetch the warrant.

Then it began. Don Bosco was searched from head to foot.

Afterwards, they went through all the furnishings, giving special attention to the wastepaper basket, but no incriminating documents came to light. Finally, aggravated by the fruitless search, the officer in charge said to Don Bosco, "Don't make us waste our time. Hand over the papers."

"What papers?"

"The ones we are looking for."

"I cannot give you what I do not possess."

"Have you no papers showing your relations with the pope and the Jesuits?"

"If ever I had them, they would long ago have been destroyed or put safely away. Now, go on with your search. As for me, I have no time to waste."

He sat down to write some letters. As soon as he finished, the officer took possession of them while the two others continued their investigation.

At one moment they thought they had something when they discovered a small box with a double lock.

"What is this?"

"It's a secret. I can't tell you," said Don Bosco gravely.

"Secret or no secret, it must be opened."

"Sorry, I will not open it. I have the right to keep documents hidden that might discredit me or my congregation. Leave that box alone."

"Open it! Otherwise, we shall smash the lock."

Don Bosco reluctantly yielded to their demand. Out of the drawer they pulled a package of bills showing that Don Bosco owed considerable sums of money to the baker Magra, the tanner who had supplied the shoemakers' workshop, and many other local merchants. There were invoices for oil, rice, macaroni and other things.

"You have been making fools of us," cried the indignant officer to Don Bosco.

"I was not trying to make a fool of you," he answered soothingly. "I did not wish you to find my debts, but you insisted on seeing and knowing everything. Never mind, if you would only pay a few of these bills you would be doing an act of charity."

Continuing their search, the police found the original text of Pope Pius IX's brief giving the papal permission for the congregation. The officer wanted to carry it away.

"I object. That is an original document. Does it matter to you if I give you an exact copy? Here's one," said Don Bosco, offering them a recent issue of Catholic Readings, the Salesian magazine.

"But this is in Italian," objected one of the men.

"Yes, but the Latin is by the side; what is more, here you have a translation of it."

"This is much better," remarked another. "Italian is easier to understand."

As their search continued, they came upon a collection of books stashed in a wardrobe. "What are these?"

"They are books written by the Jesuits," said Don Bosco.

"By the Jesuits! In that case, we will take them."

"They are lives of the saints and are very edifying," said Don Bosco. "Take this one for instance, about Saint Simeon the Stylite. It is interesting, very interesting. Listen: 'This extraordinary man, moved by the thought of hell, and knowing he had only one soul, which he must save at all costs, left his country, parents, and friends and withdrew into solitude. He lived for many years at the top of a pillar on which he had built a crude shelter. From there he preached to the multitudes, reproaching the people of the world for thinking only of their pleasures and not of the eternal punishments awaiting them for their ill use of time...' "

"That will do," interrupted the police officers testily.

"You gentlemen would be very obliging," said Don Bosco, "if you would kindly remember that it is the eve of Pentecost, and that I have several hundred boys to confess."

"We're finished," answered one of the three. But that did not stop them from seizing the evening mail when it was delivered to him.

The first letter they happened to open was from the Minister of the Interior, Louis Farini. It strongly recommended a poor orphan to the charity of Don Bosco, for whose admission His Excellency himself pledged to pay six pounds.

This was the same Minister who had signed the search warrant.

The police let their arms drop to their sides—a schizophrenic government following two policies at the same time!

In their confusion they forgot to check the rest of the correspondence. It was a good thing that they did not, for among them was a certain letter from Rome, which could have been easily distorted to cause many difficulties for Don Bosco.

Seeing this letter, Don Bosco had the presence of mind to say to the officers, "I see you are very dirty from this nasty job. Allow me to lend you this brush. You must be tired after searching for more than three hours. I will send for something to quench your thirst."

The boys playing in the yard had spent the last three hours trembling for their Father's freedom. However, when they saw a tray with a bottle and glasses go by, they knew that Don Bosco had once more turned around the very men who had been sent to do him harm.

Unexpected Help

Although Don Bosco had no lack of resourcefulness, he often received much-needed help from an unexpected source.

Don Bosco entitled the last chapter of his Memoirs "A Mysterious Dog: Grigio." There he relates how a strange gray dog protected him from time to time. The dog came to be known as Grigio, from the Italian word for 'gray.' All sorts of attempts have been made to account for this animal, which always seemed to be present whenever Don Bosco needed protection but was subsequently nowhere to be found.

Those who saw it described it as a German shepherd standing about three feet high with a ferocious appearance. The first time Don Bosco's mother set eyes on it, she cried out in alarm.

In those days the Valdocco was more isolated than it is now, and one had to cross a wide stretch of rough waste ground dotted with trees and bushes to reach the seminary. Since he had been physically attacked many times, Don Bosco was obliged to go out accompanied. One evening, however, he was returning home alone, and as he was making his way across this open area he began to feel afraid. Suddenly, a large dog bounded to his side, terrifying him even more.

"Yet its attitude was not threatening," Don Bosco writes. "It was rather like a dog that had recognized its master. We quickly became friends, and it accompanied me as far as the Oratory. That was not the only time I met it. On different occasions it kept me company, sometimes providentially.

"Towards the end of November, 1854, on a sleety night I was returning from the town. In order not to be alone I took the road leading from the Consolata down to the Cottolengo Institute. At one point I noticed that two men were walking a short distance in front of me, matching their pace with mine. I crossed over to the other side to avoid them but they did the same. I then tried to turn back but it was too late. They suddenly wheeled around and were on me in two steps. Without a word they threw some kind of coat over me. I struggled in vain to break loose. One of them then tried to gag me with a scarf. I wanted to shout but I hadn't the strength.

"At that moment Grigio appeared, growling like a bear; he hurled himself at the first man with his paws at his throat while snarling at the other. They had to let go of me to deal with the dog.

" 'Call off your dog!' they shouted, almost paralyzed with fear.

" 'I'm going to,' I replied, 'but next time leave strangers alone.'

" 'Call him off quickly!' they shouted.

"Grigio went on barking. The two thugs took off as fast as they could, and Grigio accompanied me to the Cottolengo where I stopped to recover for a moment. Then I returned to the seminary, this time well protected. Every evening when I went out alone I always noticed Grigio on one side of the road."

One evening, Grigio flatly refused to allow Don Bosco to leave the house by lying across the doorway and growling whenever he tried to pass. "If you won't listen to me, listen to the dog; it has more sense than you," remarked his mother. A quarter of an hour later a neighbor ran in to say that he had heard of a plot to assault Don Bosco that night.

When attempts to harm him ceased, the dog disappeared and was not seen again, save once. In 1883, Don Bosco arrived late one night to the station at Bordighera accompanied by one of his priests. Finding no one to show him the way, he wandered through the dark, stormy night trying to find the Salesian house. Suddenly, he was welcomed by a bark, as Grigio appeared and led him to the house.

"All sorts of stories have been told about this dog," remarks Don Bosco, "but I never discovered who its master was. I only know that throughout the many dangers I encountered, this animal protected me providentially."

In fact, Don Bosco never tried to discover whose dog it was. "What does it matter? What counts is that it was my friend."

Don Bosco

Lifetime: Born in 1815, died in 1888 at the age of 72

Order: Salesians

Founded: Turin, Italy, 1859, at the age of 44

Mission: Christian education

Impact: By his death there were 768 Salesians in 64 foundations throughout Europe and South America. Today there are thousands throughout the world.

Quote: "How can I do this, when I am only a poor ignorant boy?"

"Don't worry, I will give you someone to show you and teach you, and you will see that everything will be possible."

"At that moment I saw beside me a beautiful Lady whose garments reflected points of light like a thousand stars. She took me by the hand and said, 'Look!' I saw that in place of the boys, there were a lot of little wild animals, snapping and snarling at each other. 'This is your work,' she said, 'make yourself humble and strong. What you are about to see is what you must do.' I looked and I saw that the snarling animals had been changed into lambs, chasing each other and jumping for joy. I sighed once again and the Lady put her hand on my head and said sweetly, 'Do not worry, in good time you will understand everything.' "

BIBLIOGRAPHY

Almedingen, E.M., *St Francis of Assisi*,
Alfred A. Knopf, New York.

Auffray, A., *St John Bosco*,
Salesian Publications, Blaisdon.

Ball, A., *Modern Saints*,
Tan, Rockford, IL.

Claret, A., *Autobiography*,
Claretian Publications, Chicago.

Dempsey, M., *John Baptist de la Salle*,
Bruce, Milwaukee, WI.

Genelli, F., *Life of St Ignatius of Loyola*,
Benziger Brothers, New York.

Habig, M., ed., St Francis of Assisi:
Writings and Early Biographies,
Franciscan Herald Press, Chicago.

Jørgensen, J., Don Bosco,
Burns, Oates, and Washbourne, London.

Margaret, H., A Kingdom and a Cross: St Alphonsus Liguori, Bruce,
Milwaukee, WI.

Milcent, P., Jeanne Jugan: Humble, So As To Love More, Darton,
Longman, and Todd, London.

Miller, D.F. and Aubin, L.X., St Alphonsus Liguori:
Bishop, Confessor, Founder of the Redemptorists,
and Doctor of the Church,
Tan, Rockford, IL.

Nevin, W., Teresa of Avila: The Woman,
Bruce, Milwaukee, WI.

Peers, E., ed., The Autobiography of Teresa of Avila,
Image, New York.

Ravier, A.,
Ignatius of Loyola and the Founding of the Society of Jesus, Ignatius, San
Francisco.

Royer, F.,
The Life of St Anthony Mary Claret,
Tan, Rockford, IL.

Rushe, D.,
Edmund Rice: The Man and His Times,
Gil and McMillan, Dublin.

Thompson, F.,
St Ignatius Loyola,
Universe, London.

Thurston, H., and D. Attwater, eds.,
Butler's Lives of the Saints, Christian Classics,
Westminster, MD.

Walsh, W.T.,
St Teresa of Avila,
Tan, Rockford, IL.

❧